The Ultimate Leader

The Servant

Bishop Anthony W. Slater, Ph.D.

THE ULTIMATE LEADER, *The Servant*

TCM Publishing, Goldsboro, NC 27534

Cover Design: Roderick J. Stevenson, Kreative Koncepts (919)394-0152

Printed in the USA

Dedication

This book is dedicated to my family:

My Parents, Reginald W. Slater and Madaline L. Slater; **My Wife,** Betty Slater; **My Children,** Elijah, Emmanuel, Shaniqua Nicole, Trevand and Tracey, George and Laverne, Richard Jr. and Tyra, Tanya; **My Grandchildren,** Lanesha, Tamesha, Shaquanna, Tamika, Tanya, Richard *III,* Tony, Shawn; **My Brothers and Sisters,** Reginald Slater Jr. (*deceased*), Emery Slater (*deceased*) and Denise Slater, Eugene and Wendy Slater, Wendell and Michelle Slater, Mark Slater, Precious and Dr. Tyrone Walker, Denise and Victor Blakey

And to the men of God who have impacted my life in a way that words can not describe:

Arch-Bishop Roy E. Brown, Arch-Bishop Jesse Delano Ellis II, The late Arch-Bishop Wilbert S. McKinley, Apostle Walter L. Barbour, Bishop D. Myles Golphin, Bishop E. Bernard Jordan, Prophet Todd M. Hall, Pastor Timothy E. Harper, Prophet Frank Webster

Recognition and Gratitude

Special thanks to:

My lovely wife; *Pastor Betty Slater, who has allowed me to serve many great Men and Women of God through the years, and who has been a tremendous example of a true helpmeet.*

My wonderful staff; *Deaconess Ka-Sheena Ballard, Sister Shelli Wilson, Minister Tricia Haigler, Sister Joi Baker*

Those who I have had the privilege to serve; *Bishop D. Myles Golphin, Apostle Walter L. Barbour, Prophet Todd M. Hall*

The best group of people the Lord could have blessed me with; ***Tehillah Church Ministries****, Goldsboro, NC*

Foreword

If there was ever a time in the history of the church that leadership direction is required, it is now. If we are to segue into twenty-first century mandates, it is necessary to begin with the foot soldiers. Many ministers today desire the glamour of the position, but want no part of the struggles associated with ministry. They want to start at the top, while foregoing the training and groundwork necessary to achieve greatness. It is important in any profession to be properly trained. Unfortunately, we find that the church of today suffers due to the lack of leadership skills.

Bishop Anthony W. Slater has been given a mandate and a burden to coach and prepare selected individuals for influential servant-leadership. The one thing I have known of Bishop Slater for many years is his personal commitment to serve his superiors with dignity and respect. That is what this work can and will inculcate in those who study and apply it – they will become serious about their personal commitment to serve as unassuming servants. Bishop Slater has not only shared his expertise, but also his heart, as I have witnessed the passion he displays when he teaches on this subject.

I strongly urge every would-be and seasoned leader to work their way through the steps outlined in this instruction manual and apply the philosophy for success given for enlargement in the Body of Christ. This manual covers many areas of study that will show you character traits for successful leadership development. I have personally observed Bishop Slater move from servant to leader in the many classes he has taken under my tutoring and I am thrilled to have shared in the maturity of this great man of God for this hour.

I pray that those who study from this work will apply the lessons to help propel their ministries to become effective and productive servant-leaders for the next generation. Bishop Slater's passion is to observe wholeness in leadership and perfection in service.

Bishop D. Myles Golphin, Th.D. Ph.D.
Living In Favor Global Network

Preface

Grace and peace be unto you from God our Father and the Lord Jesus Christ! It is an honor to live in this dispensation of the Holy Spirit. We are living in a time of information with very little passion; but we do have an opportunity to show the love of God. The Holy Spirit can come upon a willing vessel and use that person to help the Man or Woman of God simply by taking care of the small things. There is a great need for those who will seek God's face for wisdom in how to bring their Leader's VISION to fruition.

I pray that this manual will provoke passion for the Body of Christ; to build the Kingdom of God, one servant at a time. The missing ingredient is LOVE, and my Bible tells me that God is love.

> *"Whoever does not love does not know God,*
> *because **God is love**." 1 John 4:8*

Bishop Anthony W. Slater, Ph.D.

Introduction

"And God hath set some in the church, first apostles, secondarily prophets, thirdly teachers, after that, miracles, then gifts of healings, helps, governments, diversities of tongues." 1 Corinthians 12:28

In this scripture, we learn that the assigned offices of ministry are: apostles, prophets, teachers, and after that miracles, then gifts and healings. Notice that the next assignments are helps, governments, and lastly diversities of tongues. Many in the Pentecostal and Charismatic churches place more emphasis on the gifts of tongues, but in this scripture, it places helps before gifts of tongues and government.

This gives the impression that the Ministry of Helps is also important. In the scriptures you will find that good leaders are needed to help run the church. In this book we will explore the beginning stages of becoming the ultimate leader.

Table of Contents

Chapter 1

The Concept of Servanthood

Servanthood is a concept which brings leader and servant together. In an effort to empower people to overcome, we must first understand what our authority is. Before you can become a leader you must first be a servant. We begin our mission in empowerment by defining authority in Christ through the covenant established by God. Webster's dictionary defines authority as the *"power to influence the behavior of others; group or person with power; an expert."* Let's explore the first definition, *"the power to influence the behavior of others"* suggests that there is a prerogative of determining or ruling in order to influence. The Hebrew term for this type of authority is *"Rabah"* which means *"to increase (in whatever respect), to bring in abundance; be in authority; continue; enlarge (more in number); make a great man; to grow"*. So, we must ask, *where is our authority*? It is in our servanthood, because one's level of authority is determined by their level of submission.

What is Covenant? Many dictionaries define covenant as, "*a formal or solemn, binding agreement*". The Hebrew word for covenant is "*Karath*", meaning "t*o make an alliance or bargain by cutting away flesh and passing between pieces; make a league.*" Our covenant is with God, but our loyalty has to be to man. The key element here is balance, which is required so that you are not so loyal to man that you miss your commitment with God. This means that it is your responsibility to stay committed to God in all that you say; keeping your vow with God as His child, submitting fully to Him. Access into another's life can be the reason for a covenant agreement, although this type covenant may not carry any authority. This is why you must remain loyal to God and also to man. Loyalty is the key to servanthood whether you are serving the Bishop, Pastor or others in ministry. In Galatians 5:13, Paul instructs the Galatians, "*Through love, serve one another.*" Our desire to serve has to begin in the heart. We cannot just move up simply because we serve in the church, this should not be our main goal.

In Ephesians 6:5-6 (the Amplified version) the church is instructed to, "*Have respect for their 'masters' or those with whom they are servants to, and to have eager concern to please them; with singleness of motive, and with all of their heart as service unto the Lord.*" This holds true for the entire Body of Christ. Paul is saying that we should serve others as if we are serving the Lord. In verse 6, Paul further states that we should not do it as if they are watching us, but as servants of Christ, doing the will of God heartily and with all of our soul. Rendering service readily with goodwill, as unto the Lord, and not unto man. As a result, we understand that we are to serve man and reverence God.

Chapter 2

Authority through Covenant

We now see the connection between keeping our covenant with God by serving those who He has placed over us. The person that you have the covenant with is the authority by which you rule. For example, if you are ordained as an Elder within a certain ministry, then you operate in authority under that ministry's covering. Not having the agreement with that leader through your service to him may hinder your right to operate in authority within that ministry, and sometimes in other ministries. In order to become a leader; one must first be a follower. Commitment and loyalty truly define the covenant that we have, and brings balance into our lives, and gives us the authority that we now have in God.

Chapter 3

Worship through Relationship

We learned earlier that the covenant that we have gives us the authority that we walk in within the Body of Christ as we serve the leader, or Man of God with love. Without love we are, *"As a sounding brass and a tinkling cymbal; we profit nothing and we are nothing"*. (1 Corinthians 13: 1-3) Another concept of servanthood is our worship, which comes through relationship. Our worship is an expression of our relationship with God. *If we have no relationship with God, how can we worship*? You cannot worship someone that you do not know, because your worship will be false. According to John 4:22-24, *"You, {Samaritans} do not know what you are worshiping, you worship what you do not comprehend. We know what we are worshiping, we worship what we have knowledge of and understand; A time will come, when the true (genuine) worshipers will worship the Father in spirit and truth (reality); for the Father is seeking just such people as these as His worshipers."*

In defining worship from the dictionary, it means *"to regard with respect or admiration; high esteem or devotion for a person; deep respect toward God."* The Hebrew word for worship is *Shachah* meaning to *"depress, (i.e. prostrate); esp. reflex in homage to royalty or God; boy (self) down, crouch, humbly beseech; make to stoop; do reverence"*. Worship builds a relationship with God, which in turn strengthens your commitment and loyalty to the one that you have been assigned to serve. We know that a relationship is defined as, *"the state of being related or connected, either by blood or natural association."* The only way that you can have true worship is to be connected, in this case, by Jesus' blood and your relationship to God.

Chapter 4

The Ministry of Helps

In the Ministry of Helps, you must be able to lay hold onto and defend. One definition is *Ontiliptus*; (Greek) *a laying hold of; apprehension, perception, objection*. You must be able to defend and understand that it is a gift. Everyone is not called to be a part of the Ministry of Helps; as it requires specific personality traits that are not found in all. The Ministry of Helps by definition is;

- **A supernatural ministry** - A servant with an anointing to serve God, through serving His leaders.
- **One who gives assistance** - Whether it is to leadership, the laity, or fellow parishioners, anyone that steps onto the church property should be bombarded with assistance by the Ministry of Helps.
- **One who lightens the load of his leaders** - In traditional churches, it is called the Pastors Aide; in the Episcopacy, it is the Adjutancy. The servant will

usually be the Adjutant Sister, the Adjutant Apostolic, or the Adjutant Chamberlain.

Let's take a moment to look at the three servant roles in the Episcopacy that I've mentioned here, to explore their duties.

1. **The Adjutant Sister** - The female who has shown faithfulness is assigned to cover the Bishop. When serving a male Bishop, there are limitations to her duties to avoid the appearance of impropriety. The Adjutant Sister has normally served for a long period of time and knows the heart of the leader; she will have his spirit, and will often wear the same color as the Bishop.

2. **The Adjutant Apostolic** - One who makes plans, ensuring that everything is in order when the Bishop arrives to an engagement. They must always be prepared; for their role is much like that of John the Baptist's role with Jesus, preparing the way.

3. **The Adjutant Chamberlain** - One who prepares the garments; making sure that they are clean, pressed, and presentable. This individual must be

prayerful because they are dealing with consecrated garments.

The Ministry of Helps is mentioned between gifts and healings and governments. The apostles and the prophets are the gifts; they hold an office, and are building the foundation. After the foundation has been built, the Ministry of Helps comes in and brings order to it, avoiding a chaotic atmosphere. The **Porter/Usher** is another part of the Ministry of Helps, who will operate with the spirit of discernment to detect what kind of spirit is operating when people come through the door. There are many days that as a Bishop, you may not want to be hugged, but that Porter, who is filled with the Spirit, will understand and minister to you simply by speaking to you. They also may know when you need love, and they will give it to you. For example, Here comes Jezebel walking through the door, *how do you deal with that spirit?* The Porter must must always be praying, and be able to isolate that spirit to make sure that it does not spread throughout the congregation.

You must be a servant before you are able to embrace the Ministry of Helps. Here are some words that deal with being a servant.

1. **Ebed (Hebrew) -** One who is a slave or servant; to be at the complete disposal of another. (Reference Genesis 24:1-67) A slave who gives up all personal rights. (1 Kings 1:9)

2. **Abed (Hebrew) -** One who works or serves in any sense. A person who tills the ground (Genesis 2:5) One who keeps or dresses the garden. (Genesis 2:15) Adam's assignment was to till the garden.

3. **Sharath (Hebrew) -** A doer of menial and insignificant tasks. Someone who does not mind doing the small stuff. This one is the hardest for proud people to move in to. (Exodus 24:13) (Numbers 11:28)

4. **Doulos (Greek) -** A love slave; a servant who willingly bonds himself to a master. The Apostle Paul uses Doulos as a description to himself to Christ. (Romans. 1:1; Philemon 1:1)

5. **Diakone/Diakia (Greek)** - The deacon to wait upon, to run errands or to serve (1 Timothy 3:10, 13) (Revelations 2:19)

The practical side of the Ministry of Helps requires a coming together of all auxiliaries to ensure that every individual who visits or attends the church, has an experience that exudes the love of God each and every time. To be effective in the Ministry of Helps, one must:

1. **Be hospitable** - (Romans 12:10-13) Everyone who is in the Ministry of Hospitality should touch the visitor at least once. If you are a part of the Ministry of Helps, you should be able to tell your Pastor something about a visitor without looking at their visitor's card. As a servant, you are going to have to move into the place where your own house is open to ministry. That means you have to clean it! *Are you appreciative of your place of refuge? How can your leader depend on you to take care of the House of God, if you will not take care of your own house?* When you invite people to your home, you should not leave them sitting in the living room while you disappear.

2. **Be not weary in well doing** - (Galatians 6:9; 2 Thessalonians 3:13) We must be careful of servanthood burnout. We cannot allow all the cares of the world to push us out of our function. When you start to feel really tired, let your leader know that you need to take a rest. Remember, in all that you do, you are doing it as unto the Lord.

3. **Maintain balance** - (Luke 10:38-42) For the married couples, don't forget to take care of your home. Women must take care of their husbands before dealing with the Ministry of Helps. Women will be required to serve men. Don't be charged with serving another man better than you have served your own husband! If you rush to get the Bishop a glass of water, then you should run at that same speed or faster when your husband asks for one. Brother, don't rush to clean the Bishop's car, and your own car is dirty. You should not serve another better than you serve your own; and don't love on anyone in the church when you don't love on your own mate. To the Singles: Don't tell your leader that you are broke, then purchase a new car costing more than you can afford to pay. You

cannot expect the church to help you in matters like this! Also, you can't eat out every time your brothers or sisters do; sometimes, you'll need to stay home and cook. To the women who are in waiting; leave some mystery for the man that is seeking you. If you show him too much, too soon, he will lose interest because he's seen all there is to you. When dealing with relationships, your ministry can be affected. There are two types of women that men are looking to encounter; the one that they can just have sex with; or the one to take home to meet their parents. *Which one will you be*? How you present yourself will determine what and who you become. You cannot hang with buzzards, then try to soar with the eagles.

4. **Serve with a Spirit of Excellence** - (Colossians 3:23; Ephesians 6:8) You must have the right attitude and and adopt cleanliness and neatness as a way of life. Check your breath for any offensive odor; wear comfortable, clean and polished shoes; and wear clothes that fit properly.

5. **Esteem others above yourself** - (Philippians. 2:3; 1 Thessalonians 5:13) No matter how great you are at

what you do, you must remain humble and modest. Even at times when you are being repeatedly complimented on your work, be careful that you don't start to believe everything that you hear about yourself and become a legend in your own mind. Bless someone with your mouth by sharing things with them; let others know how much you appreciate them.

The Purpose of the Ministry of Helps is to bring support to those who have been called to the governmental ministry. (Ephesians 11:16) The Ministry of Helps assists Apostles, Prophets, Pastors, Teachers with accomplishing what God has called them to do.

There are several primary functions;
- To perfect and to edify the Body of Christ.
- To add to God's House
- To come into the unity of the faith
- To speak the truth in love
- To grow up in Him
- To supply every joint

And several support functions;

- Prayer - You must talk to God on behalf of your leaders. When you pray for a person, it helps you to become less critical of them.
- Financial Support - The three T's: Time, Talent and Treasure.
- Hands on service - You must put your hands to work.
- Encouragement - Encouraging others to move up to higher heights in God. You pray for me, I will pray for you.
- Maintain a positive attitude - Check your attitude to be sure that your motives are pure.

The goals of the Ministry of Helps are to;

- Speak the same thing, with the same mind and judgment. All on one accord.
- Discover, develop, and deploy the spiritual gifts to every member of the Body of Christ.
- Maximize and utilize all human resources in the House of God.

- Reproduce the character of Christ in others. All should be as trees of righteousness that others can eat of the fruit thereof.

Chapter 5

The Requirements for Servanthood

1. *You must be born again* - You cannot function as a servant in the House of God without knowing Jesus as your Lord and personal Savior.

2. *You must be spirit filled* - Others must see the love of God operating in you.

3. *You must be consistent in your prayer life* - You must be faithful in prayer, at church and at home.

4. *You must live a holy lifestyle* - You cannot work at a strip club on Saturday night, then come in on Sunday morning and work in the Ministry of Helps. You will bring spirits from that sinful place with you on Sunday. You may not be possessed with a spirit, but you can be oppressed by a spirit. There are certain spirits that follow your bloodline; for example: If your grandfather was an alcoholic, you must be careful with alcohol and the intake of it. If your mother was promiscuous, you have to be careful that the spirit of lust does not creep into your generation.

5. ***You must study God's Word*** - 2 Timothy 2:15 *"Study to show thyself approved"* You must study to know who you are in Christ and to help build up the work of the ministry. David puts it this way, *"In thy word have I hid in my heart that I might not sin against thee".* When you are being tempted with or by things, you don't have time to run and get your Bible.

6. ***You must be faithful in church attendance*** – In order to be placed in a position, people need to know who you are. When a ministry is flowing, it should be like a paragraph and each department has a sentence. One department starts it, and then the other should be able to come in and finish it with a period and be able to start the next sentence.

7. ***You must be faithful in giving*** - *Will a man rob God?* It is imperative that you be a Tither on a consistent basis! *"If a man is faithful with a little, God will bless him with much".* Tithing is based on the firstfruit, which is your gross earnings.

8. ***Loyalty to leadership and their vision*** - If God requires the leader to have a vision for the House, it is your job to know what that vision is, and to get in

line with it! Whether you are single or not, you should have a vision of where you want to see yourself and your family in five years.

9. *Submit to authority* – You must be yielded to the authority of your leader; even when you don't agree with their decisions. The vision is greater than you, and your response should be obedience.

10. *Be approachable* - In the Ministry of Helps, someone should be able to approach you without reservation. The Bible says, *"The joy of the Lord is your strength"*. The enemy slips his hand into our hearts and steals our joy by messing with our money, our family, and our health. Don't allow the cares of this world to interfere with your service.

REWARDS AND BENEFITS OF SERVANTHOOD

A. The honor of God for your faithfulness. (John 12:26)

B. The blessings of your leader (Exodus 39:43) The faithful servant gets the privilege of going out and traveling with the leader; they are introduced to the right people necessary to get what they need, and to take them where they need to go.

Chapter 6

The Characteristics of a Servant's Heart

a. Compassionate (Matthew 9:35-36)

b. Willing to assist (Matthew. 8:1-3)

c. Humble (Luke 14:11; 18:14)

d. Warm (Luke 10:38-42, John 12:1-8)

e. Forgiving (Luke 15:11-32; 23:34)

f. Brokenness (John 11:33-36)

g. Charitable (also called Loving) (1 Peter 4:8-10)

h. Selfless (Romans 12:1, Acts 20:19; 26:7, 2 Peter 1:5 & 10)

Chapter 7

Beware of Servanthood Burnout

Signs of Burnout

1. Loss of zeal
2. Loss of joy
3. Lack of energy
4. Extremely sensitive
5. Quick to anger
6. Cavalier attitude
7. Forgetful
8. Too busy
9. Making excuses
10. No longer reliable
11. Avoidance
12. Broken fellowship

Servanthood Key

When better is available, your best isn't good enough.

Be careful of the spirits that haunt many ministries; they are called JEZEBEL and GRANGER. The spirit of Jezebel has nothing to do with makeup or clothing, and can apply to men or women. The Jezebel spirit is manipulative and controlling; it operates when the Bishop is upset with one person, and everyone else gets upset with that person as well. You have no right to deal with that person in the same manner your leader does.

The spirit of Granger is one of pride and conceit; you are so wonderful that no one does anything better than you. You are a legend in your own mind. Your arrogance is so repugnant that no one wants to be around you.

In dealing with hospitality, there is another spirit that can creep in, and it is called the spirit of LUST. When this spirit creeps in, what began as a friendship, can become an unhealthy connection called the soul tie. There are some people that come into the ministry that have the spirit of lust and will look to you to fulfill their desires. When working in the Ministry of Helps, you must be careful that people do not misread your friendliness as flirtation. You must be prepared to put people in their place with love if they overstep your boundaries, and be prepared to say when enough is enough. You must enforce the rules and regulations of the House, and everyone will not always like you. So when you open your mouth, be prepared to be despised.

Be careful of the spirit of WITCHCRAFT, which can begin to permeate the church, attacking the men and making them feel less than men because some women start verbally castrating them. Often you will hear a woman say, *I don't need a man*; which may be true, but it also borders on lesbianism. You will never hear a man saying that he does not need a woman. If you do, pray with him and cast that devil out! For married couples, you may be going through hell in your house, but do not think that the outside world is much better. The grass may look greener on the other side, until you step over there and find out its Astroturf.

You must beware of the transference of spirits, called *Transpneumigration*. You have to be careful that when you leave the House of God that you do not take the frustrations of the church home with you and aggravate your family. Any trouble your leaders are having in their homes should have no affect on yours.

The Ministry of Helps is, *TEAMWORK!*
The Ministry of Helps is, *UNDERSTANDING!*
The Ministry of Helps is, *LOVE*!

And ye shall know my disciples that ye have love one to another.

And the greatest among you shall be your Servant.

CHAPTER 8

To Be Carnally Minded v/s Spiritually Minded

1 Corinthians 3: 1-3 (Message version) *"But for right now, friends, I'm completely frustrated by your nonspiritual dealings, with each other and with God, Your acting like infants in relation to Christ, capable of nothing much more than nursing at the breast.. Well, then, I'll nurse you since you don't seem capable of anything more. As long as you grab for what makes you feel good or makes you look important, are you really much different than a babe at the breasts, content only when everything's going your way?"*

In times past, carnality was equated to fleshly issues, usually, fornication and adultery. However, when you begin to study the text, the word *carnal* means: *fleshly, having the nature of flesh, and being under control of the animal appetites.* Carnal also means, *being governed by mere human nature*, not by the devil, and certainly not by the Spirit of God. It also relates to depravity and being deprived.

I am not speaking of those who walk around with the Bible in their hands, feeling that they have arrived. In understanding the way ministry works, we enter in to worship, and we exit to serve. We should serve the Lord with gladness in all that we do. *How can we serve the Lord when our minds are yet carnal and not spiritual?* That is why the Bible tells us, *"Be ye transformed by the renewing of our minds. Let this mind be in you which is in Christ Jesus." Why is it necessary for us to change our minds?* Because our thinking has to be detoured from our old thought patterns.

We've just discussed the carnal, let us now talk about the spiritual. In dealing with the spiritual aspect, we are talking about *charismata*, moving with the gifts of the spirit. A good gift of the spirit is the Manger spirit, the Holy Spirit. *How do you know when someone is filled with the Holy Spirit?* You will know them by their fruit, one of which is love. You cannot know God and claim to love Him without loving others! The difference is the world is carnal in nature, but we are supposed to be spiritual, so because of this, God uses us. The Bible teaches, *"His thoughts are not like our thoughts."* The carnal man says to give hurt in return for hurt, but the spiritual man says, *I am to love them.* Most of the time, we fight battles that are not necessarily meant for us to fight, then we end up dealing with foolishness because we have become immature and carnal. If we want to see the Spirit of God move, then love must be displayed. Envy and strife have no place in the Body of Christ! Some assignments require that I am close to the elders, ministers and deacons, until they have grown strong enough to be kicked out of the nest.

There are times that I must force-feed people because some adapt to the teaching differently. In 1 Corinthians 3:3, it speaks about being *content only when things are going your way.* The moment that an individual does not like what is going on, they get an attitude. Well, there is a price to pay because if you get close enough to me, you will get laid out, one time or another. If you desire to work closely with your leader, you cannot be sensitive. The darts that are intended for the leaders will occasionally be diverted, and if you are in the way, you may get blindsided. The more you hang out with your leader, the more people are going to talk and begin thinking that you are trying to move into their position.

The scripture says, *"He called us out of darkness into the marvelous light"* to show forth His praises. When you do not show forth praises unto God, you are canceling out your purpose. The Catechism says, the chief end to man is to worship God and enjoy Him forever. *How can you enjoy God if you continue to be envious of other relationships*? We have some people who are jealous when a married couple are having a good time and others are not. There are married women who are jealous of single women. Husband and wives are fighting over foolishness and jockeying for position because neither of them know who they are. We don't have time to fight one another when the enemy is wreaking havoc in the world and the church! So, carnal minds have hindered us from being true servants of God.

Let us look at the great leaders of our day, some boast of how many adjutants they have. Understand that adjutant is a military term from the 17th Century, and it means to assist one in high command. An armor bearer is another word for squire and it means one who helped. In today's era, armor bearers are carrying the Bibles, protecting, and making sure that their leaders have everything they need. I am training more armor bearers to lend and help serve other ministries; when other Bishops or pastors come in, I can dispatch an armor bearer who can be trusted to serve them well. A good armor bearer knows when to keep his mouth shut, but is not afraid to stand up and approach people. If sickness comes upon their leader, they need to be able to pray against that sickness; or if someone comes against their leader to do harm, they can begin to pray against it because they have the spirit of discernment. When you become a worshiper at Tehillah Church Ministries, you are signing up to war; we intend to take back everything that the enemy has stolen from us. The Bible says that *"the wealth of the wicked is laid up for the just"*, and our leaders are looking for those who are going to be obedient and trust God at His word; who have the word of God in their mouths, a praise on their lips, and a dance in their feet. The Bible says that you should never receive an evil report about an elder, so, whether it is true or not is irrelevant. What happens is our minds become poisoned and you start looking at that person differently because of your carnal thinking.

Romans 8:1

There is therefore now no condemnation to them which are in Christ Jesus, who walk not after the flesh, but after the Spirit.

We have to remember that everything negative that is happening is not necessarily the devil. We have to see with our spiritual eyes so we don't miss God. For instance, I always tell my leaders, "*I do or say nothing just to be doing or saying it*". If I were to put someone in a bad situation, you can believe there's a good reason for it. If I give someone an assignment and then lay them out, I have a good reason for it. I may lay you out publicly in front of your peers and wait to see if your attitude changes which will tell me whether or not you are ready for what I have to give, because people need to see that you can handle rebuke. *How can you lead, and not receive from your leader?* If you are in the military and they start to yell at you, you can't tell them to stop unless you want to risk getting kicked out. We have to stop running around in our Sunday clothes when we should be wearing our fatigues!

The Body of Christ is at war and the enemy is gaining ground because our soldiers are having trouble running in their dress shoes!

I recently spoke with a minister living in another state who shared with me that the church she attends was going on a fast. She stated that she did not feel like fasting, and she did not have the heart to do it. I asked her what was she going to do; to which she replied that she understood that it was a sacrifice to fast but she just did not feel like doing it. I informed her that the fast was not about feelings or sacrifice, but it is about obedience. It has nothing to do with meat, its about your willingness to listen. *If you cannot be trusted with a little, how can God trust you with much*? That is like saying, *Lord, if I had a million dollars, I would build the Cathedral*! You are a liar because, if you cannot be trusted to tithe off one hundred dollars, you surely won't tithe off one million! *Do you realize that in the days of old people lost their lives for the gospel*? People were beheaded because they were talking about the scriptures. In the days of old, they had to sneak around so that they could praise God and read the Bible, and here we are, able to worship and read whenever we feel like it, but we're complaining.

Romans 8:2

For the law of the Spirit of life in Christ Jesus hath made me free from the law of sin and death.

The problem is, as carnal minded Christians we are still bound according to the scriptures, *"For where the spirit of the Lord is there is liberty"*. So, when we come to church on Sunday morning bound with no freedom, that means that we have not trusted God to free us. We also have not embraced the truth because the Bible says that *"the truth shall make you free"*.

Romans 8:3

For what the law could not do, in that it was weak through the flesh, God sending his own Son in the likeness of sinful flesh, and for sin, condemned sin in the flesh:

Jesus was the perfect gift and came as sin for us, so when He died on the cross, He laid his life down for us. The Bible tells us *where there is no shedding of blood;*

there will be no remission of sin. This is the ultimate sacrifice, and the greatest love of them all. *Can you imagine God asking for your child, like Isaac?* Most of us would be torn to pieces because many are even afraid to send their child to school for fear that they will bump their head or scratch their knee! The Bible states that "*they were born and shaped in sin and iniquity*". It doesn't matter what you teach at home, when they get out there in the world, there is a greater influence. The principle that you have to hold on to is that you believe God because they are exposed to things that would make you vomit. Just visit some of these grade schools, or look on the internet and see what some of these children are doing. There are websites that show kids holding a beer bottle at five years old!

Romans 8:4

That the righteousness of the law might be fulfilled in us, who walk not after the flesh, but after the Spirit.

I always teach in my home, *the thing you feed the most, will grow the most. Well, what are you feeding yourself? What are you doing in your spare time? If you are dealing with the spirit of depression, what are you*

43

doing to get that spirit off of you? Strife, envy, and hanging around people who do not speak positive things into your life are friends of depression. You should desire to be around those who can encourage you. I spoke with a preacher once about a situation that I was dealing with and his response to me was: *Have you ever thought about just closing the doors of the church? They made you a Bishop, but maybe you were not ready because your people are acting up. Why don't you just give in?* I foolishly began to think that he was right; but, after giving it some thought, I remembered that misery loves company. *How can two walk together unless they agree?* He began dealing with my flesh which made me think things that I had never thought of before. I was on the brink of interrupting my purpose by listening to that man. But, I did the same thing that David did; I encouraged myself. I preached a message once titled, "Kiss and say goodbye", which is exactly what I did with him, and I no longer speak to him.

Romans 8:5-6

For they that are after the flesh do mind the things of the flesh; but they that are after the Spirit the things of the Spirit.

For to be carnally minded is death; but to be spiritually minded is life and peace.

What are you after? You often will hear people say, *I am not happy with my life*, but what are they thinking about? The Bible says that the joy of the Lord is my strength; so if you have no joy, then your strength is depleted. You may ask, *how do you build your strength?* In the presence of God through your praise and worship! He is looking for you to throw up your hands and say, *Thank you Lord, I praise you for continuing to have my health, and when a job opens up, I will have it.* Sometimes God will put you in a corner by making you take a position that you do not want in order to fulfill your duty. You will find men complaining about the jobs they have, but they must do that job until another door opens, because they have responsibilities. There were many instances when I wanted to quit my job as a fireman; every time the tone went off for a fire, we'd go out, extinguish the fire, then return to the station with black soot all over us. I would blow my nose and see black soot coming from it; I was too clean for all that. But, I knew I had to work because if I didn't work, we wouldn't eat and I would have to look in my wife's face waiting for an explanation. Once I joined the union, I became a Chaplain, but I did my job so well that they promoted me to union president. I even almost lost my job because I dared to do something that others would not do; I was one of the principal forces behind the city building a new two million dollar fire station. I was driving a fire truck one day, and I pressed the brakes, and they didn't work; I complained and the city had to purchase a brand new fire truck. After that, they transferred me to a station where there were not many workers, this gave me an opportunity to study, minister, and give the Word of the Lord to many people. There were people coming to the station seeking counseling while I was in my fireman's uniform. I was doing what I was meant to do until God opened the door so that I could step into my purpose.

Romans 8:7-8

Because the carnal mind is enmity against God: for it is not subject to the law of God, neither indeed can be. So then they that are in the flesh cannot please God.

When you are operating in the flesh, you cannot please God because your flesh is corrupted.

Romans 8:9

But ye are not in the flesh, but in the Spirit, if so be that the Spirit of God dwell in you. Now if any man has not the Spirit of Christ, he is none of his.

What is the spirit of Christ? The Bible says that God is love. The true essence of what God has done is, He gave His only begotten son, the greatest gift which was love, Agape. Agape is not what you feel, but it is behavioral. You cannot tell me that you love me but you will not take care of me. Many people will only love you when it is beneficial to them. This is found not only in relationships, but in the church as well. I don't tell my wife everything that goes on because if she knew some of the things that people have done against me, she would be putting Vaseline on her face and pulling her hair up! Once you mess with her family, the fight is on! God is not through with her yet! If Christ be in you the body is dead because of sin, but the spirit is life because of righteousness.

(Romans 8:6-8 Message Bible)

How does God get your attention? He lets drama come your way so you will pray more. When it is time to praise

47

and worship, you will just sit there when things are going well for you; but let your lights get cut off; you will have no problem praising and worshiping! I spoke earlier about almost getting fired from the fire department; when that happened, I began to pray and the Lord heard my cry. I was laid prostrate before the Lord in hopes that I would not lose my job because they had every right to let me go because I was speaking against authority. The Bible says in Romans 13:1-2 *"Let every soul be subject unto the higher powers. For there is no power but of God: the powers that be are ordained of God. Whosoever therefore resisteth the power, resisteth the ordinance of God: and they that resist shall receive to themselves damnation."* Remember, Greater is He that is within you, than He that is in the world.

2 Corinthians 10:1-4

Now I Paul myself beseech you by the meekness and gentleness of Christ, who in presence am base among you, but being absent, am bold toward you:

(He is identifying himself by the attributes of the man of God Himself)

But I beseech you, that I may not be bold when I am present with that confidence, wherewith I think to be bold against some, which think of us as if we walked according to the flesh.
For though we walk in the flesh, we do not war after the flesh:

For the weapons of our warfare are not carnal, but mighty through God to the pulling down of strong holds; Casting down imaginations, and every high thing that exalteth itself against the knowledge of God, and bringing into captivity every thought to the obedience of Christ;

We are fighting against each other in the flesh, but the problem is the spirit! When Peter came up against Jesus; Jesus did not say, *I rebuke you Peter*, He said *"Satan, the Lord rebuke you."* He was not dealing with the flesh, but He was dealing with the spirit that is within. If we learn to deal with the spirit that is behind our trouble instead of a person, we will stop bothering each other. (2 Corinthians 10:4 Message version) *The tools of our trade aren't for marketing or manipulation, but they are for demolishing that entire massively corrupt culture.*

49

So what are we doing? We are playing pity-pat with the devil instead of dealing with the powers of darkness. When I meet someone for the first time I am not looking to see how beautiful they are, or how long their hair is; I am trying to find out who they are. We have to get our minds off of the flesh and start looking to God. We say that we trust God, but we do not trust Him in every area of our lives. Some of the leaders that I had last year, will not make it this year; I won't have to disqualify them, they will disqualify themselves. When it is time to do what God has called them to do, if they have not spent time with Him, they are going to give up the ghost.

CHAPTER 9

Transpneumigration

1 Timothy 5:22

Do not be hasty in the laying on of hands, and do not share in the sins of others. Keep yourself pure.

To define transpneumigration etymologically, *Trans* means to go from one place to another, such as transportation; *Pneuma* means spirit; *Migration* means to establish new residence. So, when your leader lays hands on someone, he or she is transferring something, and you have the ability to receive what you desire. If the person laying hands on you is an angry, yet anointed person, you can ask the Lord to allow you to be imparted with their spirit of worship, but not their spirit of anger. As the porter of your own body and spirit, you decide what comes in and what goes out; for it is not what goes into a man that defiles him, but what comes out. So, if you start using profanity, understand that it was already in you.

Wisdom Key

When you discover that God has made you, you will take the limits off God in your life.

Sometimes we hinder God because He believes in you, but YOU do not believe in yourself.

Happiness will never come by having the life of others; your life is for you.

When your your leader has speaking engagements, if you stay home instead of traveling with him, but later ask others about the service; you have just made yourself miserable, plus, you may have missed your moment.

Why do I feel the way I do?

(Could it be the people I am around?)

1. **Family** - There will be some people in your family that you don't need to be around. Some of your family members remind you of your former self; and they will not allow you to become the new you. Every time you are around them, they provoke you to do and say things that are not a part of the new you. Each time you are in their presence, you give an opportunity for them to whisper negative things into your ear.

2. **Friends (Platonic and Love Relationships)** - Your boy, your homie, or your crew may be fun, but you know they have lots of foolishness on their minds. Ladies, you claim that you have a male *friend*, but he may be thinking about something else; because once you entertain carnal conversations, your *friend* will be looking for sex. The friendship may start out pure, but the moment you start looking and smelling good, their thoughts and feelings for you change. Your relationships with your girlfriends

must also be watched carefully; *What do you talk about when you are together*? For me, I am a Bishop with a cross, and I know that there are some people that I can't hang around, because they remind me of my past when I was out having a blast. Your flesh will crave what you used to do; you have to take charge of your life. There are some relationships that we have entered into that we should never have been in, but we settled. The pastor told you to wait to get married, because the man that you were dating wasn't ready. But, you didn't listen and you married a boy instead of a man. While you're trying to figure out how the bills are going to be paid; he wants to know the football score. Men grow by watching other men, and I try to show the men something other than what they have been taught. You can never make a relationship right if you keep trying to cut corners; it may be wonderful for the moment, but something is going to blow up.

3. **Your environment** - You cannot be in the club *dropping it like it's hot*, then come to church with

that same spirit. For example, I had a Saint ask me once, *Why are the musicians playing secular music in the sanctuary?* I immediately called the Minister of Music into my office to discuss why this was happening. You will entreat spirits into the atmosphere that should not be around. You cannot be possessed by an evil spirit as a Christian, but oppression can take place. *Have you ever been around someone who was depressed and your spirit began to diminish and try to shut down?* That is what the spirit of oppression can do.

4. **The Internet** - *What websites are you visiting?* Often, when pornographic websites are visited, it generates links to other illicit websites by creating popups to entice you to visit them. Many of these popups are continual and cannot be taken off your computer. Those derogatory pictures stay in your mind and can create a stronghold. If you are married, you will begin to compare your spouse to what you have seen on the computer. Pornography is a spirit, and the Holy Spirit is the only thing that can separate you from it. Your flesh does not want

to give it up, so you will need help to be delivered from it.

Go where the eagles gather

You can never soar with eagles hanging out with chickens. You must ask yourself, *Where are the people I'm hanging with going*? In Amos 3:3 it states, "*How can two walk together unless they agree*". So, you must be in agreement on something, because if my brother has something that I don't, I am going to ask how he got it.

Wisdom Key

Qualify the relationships in your life.

Those with a sense of urgency get more done, and also do it on time. While others get an assignment and take their time about doing it. In high school, if your teacher gives an assignment and it's turned it in late, usually points will be taken away. But, if you do this in college, the professors will not accept the assignment at all, and you will not receive a grade for it. A true servant takes every assignment personal and to heart; so it will be carried out with precision, grace, and honor because the servant understands that the work is to the Glory of God.

During a consecration service for the Bishopric, the candidate must lay prostrate on the floor. Once they are on the floor, the other Bishops begin to surround him/her and lay hands on them, however, none of them are to lay hands on the candidate's head. Although these are prominent men and women of good report, the head is reserved for the father of the candidate because when laying hands, there is transference of spirits. In the movie *"Fallen"* featuring the actor Denzel Washington, there was a spirit that was passed from person to person by touch. You could tell when the spirit had been transferred because everyone who was touched began singing the same song, *"Time is on My Side"*. At times I wonder about the mindset of today's script writers, because some movies are very close to the reality of spiritual things!

Many have accused cartoons of having subliminal messages, but I'm not here to bash cartoons or tell you not to permit your children to watch them, because often those who make such accusations are simply being fanatical.

57

However, as parents you need to closely monitor what your children watch on television, and limit the amount of time they spend watching, because there is a transference taking place, remember, our eyes are gates. Men are creatures of sight, and if we stare at anything too long, we will begin to covet it. Titus 1:15 states; *"to the pure, all things are pure, but to those who are corrupted and do not believe, nothing is pure. In fact, both their minds and consciences are corrupted"*. Here is what the enemy will do; he begins to use a pure avenue so that the flesh will respond. It does not matter how spiritual you think you are, know that the devil has traps set in your midst!

The local church

The local church should be a microcosm of the universal Body of Christ. The church that I pastor does not look like the Body of Christ because there are no Caucasians, nor Asians in the church. The Body of Christ has all nations involved, so we have not done an ample job in reaching the lost at all costs. Just because people talk differently does not mean that they do not belong; the Bible tells us that we are a peculiar people (which means purchased, not weird), a holy nation, and a royal priesthood which is not set aside for any particular race. We are one body and when you look out into the church, you should see a picture of Jesus Christ. If the devil can keep us divided and fighting among ourselves, that leaves him free to wreak havoc on the world! God is going to call upon us to reach the ones that society has thrown away, and we as the Body of Christ must show them something different. The local church is a seed pre-program to extend the borders of God's ever increasing kingdom throughout the earth. We are seeds that were meant to grow into a tree of righteousness where the fruit of the spirit will grow. The problem is, we have been eating our own fruit, which was not meant for you, but for the one that you are married to, your co-worker, and the one sitting or standing next to you! When you are going through, allow someone else to see some long suffering, and meekness. Meekness is having the ability to do a thing, but choosing not to.

In the book of Genesis, God says, *"Adam where are you?"* As a man, Adam had to take his place and do what God said, which is why God came looking for him, because he received the directions, not Eve. Adam had to accept responsibility for his disobedience and stop blaming Eve.

When you are at work, how do you respond when you know your supervisor is crazy? How is your response different from that of the sinner? Do you blow up and curse them out, too? You must understand that we must respond, not react. Serving is not easy, so you must have the fruit called patience.

Amos 3:3

Do two walk together unless they have agreed to do so?

Proper development and plurality of leadership is something that we don't tend to see in a congregational church as much as in a connectional church. In my church, I have tiers of leadership: Pastor, Board of Elders, Deacons, Ministers, Armor Bearers, and Adjutants. Their assignment is to carry the vision, and in order to do this, they must have my spirit. Therefore, I laid hands on each of them at one time or another, so they would have the spirit of excellence, and discernment. Additionally, they must also have the spirit of adventure and be willing to try new things. If I travel overseas and one of them accompanies me; when it's time to eat, they cannot insult that culture by turning their nose up at their food.

Elders

Elders are those who have proven themselves to be faithful in attendance, in their tithes and offerings, and in being there when needed.

Ministers

The ministers are those that I recognize to have gifting in them, or those who have come to me and stated that they have been called to the ministry. God always exposes the ministers for who they really are before they are to go before the people and preach, because every minister in the House of God is not a preacher. The shepherd has a responsibility to discern in this area.

Deacons

Deacons are ministers on another level as the word minister means to serve. All of us are ministers in God's own way, just not ordained. Deacons come from the Greek word *Diakonos*. Their primary function is to serve the elders, who in turn serve the pastor. This means they are to help *run* the church; not take over the church, nor wait on the pastor and elders hand and foot.

Hospitality

Hospitality is important because the scripture requires that we be given unto it. When a visitor comes in, we should make them feel like they are the most important person on earth.

Department Leaders

Department leaders are being tested to see if they can bring progressive change to the organization they lead. Their fruit will demonstrate who they really are. It is the task of the Senior Pastor to nurture the development of his leaders by spending time with them. When that is done, there is a mentoring process taking place. This does not take place while one sees their leaders at the church, but when one-on-one time is spent in a different surrounding. It is the job of your leader to provoke you; your mentor should be sandpaper to your character, getting on your nerves and stretching you.

I have gotten many messages after preaching from people who have felt that I was preaching about them. I hear God, and the Holy Spirit reveals to me what needs to be said! Someone needs to be under conviction, and I do not have to tell you that you are going to hell. No, you just need to get your life together!

CHAPTER 10

The Impartation

Wisdom Key

Impartation and change begins with the laying on of hands

There are certain times that we must begin to pray and lay hands on people to impart and bring about change. Leaders pray for those who he/she has selected, or God has given them the unction to select to move to the next level. Now, if God tells me that one of my ministers is getting ready to move in ministry, the anointing that is in my life will be transferred onto them. Not all of it, but what I designate to send, if that person is willing and ready to receive it. Many people tell me that they want to be able to prophesy like me, but they do not understand what I had to go through. When I hear and see things and am able to pick up someone else's spirit, my heart begins to get heavy. As a shepherd, I have to watch over my sheep by prayer and in times of fasting. You must keep your leadership in prayer; this also includes the elders, ministers, and deacons.

Wisdom Key

The oil was used to anoint, but man was used to appoint.

It doesn't matter how anointed you are, you are not released to do anything until your leader activates you. You have to be sure that you are in line with the flow of the spirit. Evidence of a foul spirit is when it goes against the grain of everything else that is happening. For instance, everyone is worshiping, then someone runs to the front of the church spinning around like a top. Immediately, your spirit should say *hold it*. There are some people that will do things to distract attention from God by placing it on themselves. This is why I have a problem when people run from the back of the church to the front to dance, saying they caught the Holy Ghost. To me, that is flesh on display, because the same anointing that is in the front of the church, is also in the back. If you don't have enough room, maybe you need to change your dance. You do not go to a ballroom and break dance! The Bible says "*praise Him in the dance*", but it didn't specify which one! Just do it from your heart.

Wisdom Key

Your mentor sees further than you

How many times have you been mentored by someone who warned you about something, and you ignored them, resulting in your doing something out of character? I personally mentor most of the my leaders, and I have warned some of them about some things, and they did not listen, so the situation hit them upside their head. Sometimes, God will reveal things to your leader that He will not disclose to you. Or, God might divulge one part to your leader and the other part to you, because remember, prophecy comes in parts. When I was consecrated as a Bishop, there was a part in the service where I was surrounded by 15 Bishops who imparted their anointing upon me. I was laid prostrate on the floor with my right sock and shoe off, and the one place that the Bishops were not to lay hands on was my head, for it is reserved for the father who is putting his seal upon me. (Hebrews 6:1-3)

In my house, I prescribe baptism in the water and in the Holy Ghost, which are sacraments. In my house, we hold to three sacraments; baptism, communion, and anointing. The oil is symbolic of the Holy Spirit, but there is no power in the oil, it is only symbolic. I have seen on television that they have miracle spring water and they try to justify that biblically. This is only to get your money, and there will be letters asking for more money to follow. We have to be careful of these gimmicks; for the Bible warns in Ephesians 4:14 of *"being tossed to and fro by every wind and doctrine"*. I see too many people jump from church to church chasing the most popular prophet of the week. But, the most appalling thing about it is, some of these prophets are really anointed, but the money issue has clouded their view. I was once rebuked by a prophet because I did not set a fee for the people that were being prophesied to. I told him that he did not have the authority, and this is not the way that I live, because God holds me accountable for what I do and say. I also told him, if you want to charge for prophecy, my people will have no part of it. I may have lost a good friend and much money that he could have gotten for me over the years; but my integrity is not for sale.

Now as we were talking about imparting and the laying on of hands, during a part of the consecration, the Bishops used a Shofar to pour the oil onto my head. The Shofar is symbolic that the anointing is from God and not from an earthly vessel. Once that is done, transpneumigration takes place to the point that when I teach, my father gets excited because he sees the fruit of his labor. I get excited when I come into the house and I see my children worshiping because that is what we teach in our House. I should never have to come in and command one of my children to praise and worship God, because I know if they are not praising, then they are not obeying the scripture either. I teach, *You cannot lead unless you read.* You have to know the scripture before you can witness to someone, because you will be questioned on what you say. People who are unsaved will begin to quote more scriptures than you know, so you must be prepared. 2 Timothy 2:15 says *Study to show thyself approved unto God, a workman that needeth not to be ashamed, rightly dividing in the word of truth.*

What is the purpose of impartation?

(Leviticus 16:20-22) *"And when he hath made an end of reconciling the holy place, and the tabernacle of the congregation, and the altar, he shall bring the live goat: And Aaron shall lay both his hands upon the head of the live goat, and confess over him all the iniquities of the children of Israel, and all their transgressions in all their sins, putting them upon the head of the goat, and shall send him away by the hand of a fit man into the wilderness: And the goat shall bear upon him all their iniquities unto a land not inhabited: and he shall let go the goat in the wilderness."*

I am standing in the gap to pray for the sheep, as is my responsibility; I am taking all their burdens to the Lord. Now if my sheep have good sense, they will be praying also, and we can touch and agree. Just because I don't say anything to you, it does not mean that I am not praying for you. I know more than you think, remember, your mentor can see further than you.

The impartation of anointing

(I Samuel 16:13) *"Then Samuel took the horn of oil, and anointed him in the midst of his brethren: and the Spirit of the Lord came upon David from that day forward. So Samuel rose up, and went to Ra'mah."*

Samuel went to Ra'mah, the place of training. So, now that you are anointed, it does not mean that you have arrived, you must still be taught. It does not matter how much I like you, you must be trained.

The impartation of healing

(Acts 8:7) *"For unclean spirits, crying with loud voice came out of many that were possessed with them: and many taken with palsies, and that were lame, were healed."*

There was a great joy after the miracles took place. Now, the joy of the Lord is our strength and we are seeing the scriptures come alive as healings and impartations take place.

Impartation of spiritual gifts

(Romans 1:11-12) *"For I long to see you, that I may impart unto you some spiritual gift; to the end ye may be established: that is, that I may be comforted together with you by the mutual faith both of you and me."* In this scripture you see power of agreement.

(1 Corinthians 12:3-4) *"Wherefore I give you to understand, that no man speaking by the Spirit of God calleth Jesus accursed: and that no man can say that Jesus is the Lord, but by the Holy Ghost. Now there are diversities of gift, but the same spirit."*

Now when I am ministering, my sheep and I should be on one accord because we are under the same spirit. You have to take time to get what I have. Now, I do not have a whole lot, but what I do have cost me something! The anointing will cost you some sleep, peace, and money; because your money will show your faithfulness. For where your heart is, your treasure will be also. It is possible for people who are filled with homosexuality, greed, lust and other perverse spirits to impart their spirits upon you. *So, what about the homosexual that says they*

71

are Christian? *What about those with lust and greed?* That's all the same spirit. *Are they not saved or do they have an issue called sin?* Sin begins in your mind. *Whatsoever a man thinketh, so is he.* This is why we cannot talk about certain things with everyone. Single and married women should not be in conversation about sex or marriage unless it is done in purity and in the Word. Married women, stop telling women what goes on between you and your husband in the bedroom, because the moment you turn your back, an appetite can easily come up. Men are just ridiculous when it comes to someone looking at their woman. This is why men are so funny about the way their wives dress; it all ties in with the spirit of oppression.

Have you ever seen the cartoons where there is an angel on one shoulder and the devil on the other? The angel represents the spirit of the Lord that is in you; the devil represents your flesh, because it is greedy and cries out to be satisfied. It is up to you to decide who you will listen to; you may think that you have been faithful, *but what were you thinking about yesterday? What were you thinking when you saw Morris Chestnut walk across the screen with no shirt?* When speaking of impartation, this is why we must protect our gates (eyes). Look at what you have exposed your children to; if you and your spouse are having a disagreement in their presence, that spirit of anger can transfer. The vision statement of Tehillah Church Ministries is "*Empowering People to Overcome*", because we all have something that we need to overcome.

Money management is a problem in the Kingdom. We do not want to give in, but the moment something happens, you run to borrow money from someone else or go to the paycheck advance place. We should not support paycheck advance establishments because this puts you in a bigger bind.

1 Timothy 4:14) "*Neglect not the gift that is in thee, which was given thee by prophecy, with the laying on of the hands of the presbytery.*"

The transfer of anointing and spiritual gifts takes place during ordinations. At one time, one of my elders made a mistake and was on the sideline, but when he was restored, his anointing was greater than ever before because I released a new anointing upon him to do a work. *Have you ever had something that got ripped and had to be sewn back together*? The place that you have stitched is stronger than the rest of the material because you have made reinforcements in that area. Yes, you have made some mistakes, but once you are delivered, every area in your life will be stronger and God can use you again. That is why the Bible says *"Count it all joy when you find yourself in diverse temptations".* The Bishop or Pastor does not have to have all the answers. You have been taught, now go and teach others; this is known as the law of duplication.

Wisdom Key

Obedience proceeds success.
Sow a seed, reap a harvest.
Wealth is found in the strength of a plan.
When you fail to plan, you plan to fail.

CHAPTER 11

The Anointed Servant

In this chapter, we will explore what the anointing really is. When one is being elevated to the Bishopric, the first garment is called the cassock, which is the servant's garment, which signifies that above all else, we must first be a servant. Regardless of the heights that are reached in the Kingdom, that individual must always be a servant first. We find that some have been promoted who think that they are supposed to be served, but, when you are anointed and know who you are in the kingdom, you recognize that it is the grace of God that keeps us in the place that we are in.

One of the things that jarred my heart when writing about this topic is that many of you have been serving your leaders and you have begun to have dreams and sometimes find yourselves feeling heavy. If you are really close to your leader, you will find yourself getting angry because of the way that they are treated by others.

Dedication of Aaron and his sons

(Exodus 29:7) *"Then shalt thou take the anointing oil, and pour it upon his head, and anoint him"*.

There are several things that you have to consider when the anointing is flowing. If you want the spirit of your leader, you must first be in the right position. The Bible states that the anointing runs down, and it came down Aaron's beard. For example, if I have a speaking engagement in Raleigh, NC, and my adjutant decides to go and hear another pastor preaching somewhere else; my adjutant may be blessed by the other ministry, but he will never receive the oil that is coming from my life. So, you cannot tell me that you have my spirit and not show up for Bible study.

You also need to pray for your leaders; the more you pray, the less critical you will be of them. As you grow closer to your leader, you will at times receive the brunt of a situation that has nothing to do with you personally. Imagine that I have just had a business meeting with an associate who really rubbed me the wrong way; and my administrator comes in asking me if I'd like a soda. I'm still upset from the earlier meeting, so I yell at her. *What does she do?* Her feelings are hurt, she starts to cry, tells me I was mean to her, and decides to quit. Now, this outcome should be different if she has the spirit of her leader. She should know that it is out of character for me to act rudely, and she will understand that I am dealing with something that has nothing to do with her. Sometimes, you have to do like David did and encourage yourself by going into your secret closet to pray. But, you should think before you speak, because your flesh may rise up and decide to retaliate, instead of discerning that the leader's verbal attack is not directed at you personally. By biting her tongue, and growing thicker skin, she will continue to respect me by keeping me in my position as the man of God, and she can receive what the Lord has put into me.

The anointing

Anointing comes from a Hebrew word called *Mishchah,* which means consecrated portion, anointing oil, ointment, anointing portion, used to consecrate by anointing. An example that I've often used is; *Have you ever been to a pig picking or seen a pig being cooked on the grill?* When the pig is on the grill, once the heat hits it, the fat on the pig begins to liquify, or change to oil, which drips onto the coals or wood causing the fire to flare up.

Spiritual aspect

When you are created to feed someone, there are nutriments inside of you that can only be brought out by circumstances that you may initially see as negative. God allows these situations to take place in your life to bring the oil out of you. Show me a Christian that is not going through something and I will show you someone who is not a true Christian, because the Bible clearly tells us that we will have problems, *"Many of the afflictions of the righteous"* but the key part of this scripture is *"But God delivers us from them all"*. *Is it possible that what you are going through is designed to help you help someone else*? When the heat gets turned up on you, that is the signal for you to pray and start to worship. The Bible says *"For when the spirit of heaviness comes upon us to put on the garment of praise"*. For when we praise God, *"He inhabits the praises of His people"*. When you begin to understand praise, it will set you up for the anointing because your spirit is open. This is why we have worship and praise before the Word comes forth, because it opens up your spirit so that the preacher can pour into you.

The oil

When we look up the word oil, it basically means fat. With the olive, you must first crush it in order to retrieve the oil. God is getting the best out of you through the pain. Sometimes we are attacked by the ones that are closest to us, usually our families. Fat was designed to insulate you. The Bible talks about the oil of gladness, so when one is oily, every time the enemy tries to grab you, he cannot keep you because you are too slippery. *What are you doing to get yourself oily?*

Most of the time we come to church, we have our armor on because we are expecting someone to irritate us. But, you cannot get into worship wearing your armor. You must remove the armor to embrace the love. When you remove your armor, you still need some protection and that protection is in the oil. You should be oily when you get to church and that is why you need to have your own devotion at home, or in the car before service. Then, when the man or woman of God comes up, you are already excited about the Word because it is a part of you. You are the vessel that God wants to use, and understand that by being an anointed servant there is a crushing, a fire, and a burning involved. As a firefighter, the first thing we learned in academy was when enter into a fire, get to our knees. This parallels with the spiritual, when things get hot, get on your knees and pray! I am reminded of a Greek word, *proskenuo,* which means to bow down and kiss the very foot of. This tells you that in the midst of all that you are going through, one of the keys is to get into worship if you want the anointing to be upon you.

You must begin to understand that music changes things. Back when I was growing up, if we wanted some action, all we had to do was put on some Marvin Gaye or Teddy Pendergrass, because music changes the atmosphere. There is a good anointing and a bad anointing. If you have ever witnessed a Michael Jackson concert, people were falling all over the place. *Whose anointing does your power come from*? People say if you really want to know the real person, get them into a tight spot and see what happens. One night, I was home with my wife and I stubbed my toe. When this happened to me, I began speaking in tongues. My wife began to laugh at me knowing that I wanted to say something else because that thing really hurt. I always say that the thing you feed the most, will grow the most. Speaking in tongues is what came out first, so I am saying that whatever is in you will come out of you. I do not believe it when people say *"it slipped"*, when they curse. The Bible states it this way, *"Whatsoever a man thinketh, so is he."* This scripture kills many excuses.

Pour

Are you the vessel that allows yourself to be poured into? Are you making yourself available to be poured into? Pour means to let flow, cast, and to send forth. *Who are you hanging out with?* People can influence you to go to another place, rather than be in the place to get your blessings. God allows some people to be in your life to test your love for Him, because what is in you, is going to come out. In some traditional churches, where the pastors are voted in, it is very difficult for them to pour into the spirits of the people who are submitted to them. For example, I come into a new church to pastor where another pastor has just finished serving for 12 years. Well, I come in and I am on fire, and I get these same people that have the former pastor's spirit and try to teach them. But, they will not receive me because they are still with him. Before they are able to receive my spirit, they must first release his.

Then, we have those who are transplanted from other churches, whose opinions from their former church must die. You have to receive the spirit of your new leader to become a true anointed servant. When you get into the position where you understand that your leader is there to pour into you, then you position yourself as a yielded vessel. Most of us are cracked vessels in need of healing when we first come to church. If you are familiar with a potter's wheel, you are aware that when they place the clay on the wheel, they slam it down to remove the air bubbles. When that is done, they begin to form the clay as it is yet spinning. Well, you are that clay on God's wheel, and He is still making you by sending leaders such as apostles, prophets, pastors and teachers. My title is Bishop, which is my assignment, but I am a pastor. Therefore as a pastor, there is some nurturing and a desire inside of me to help people; there is some care and love in me to be shared. Some have sat under apostles who were not nurturers, and it was not a good experience because instead of taking time with you, their answer to any question was, *What does the Bible say*? To be an anointed servant, you must understand the gift that you are connected to, and keep them informed of what's happening in the church. Sometimes the servant knows things before the leader, because they are in the midst of the people. I spoke with a leader once who said, if you have someone on your staff that knows of something that can negatively affect the church and they do not inform the leader, that is grounds for termination. This shows that this individual is more loyal to the people, than to the leader.

We have to be in position to receive mending and at times to be the mender. Your leader may go through something and his issue becomes exposed; you as an anointed leader must put pressure on that cracked vessel. If you have an anointing, know that it can heal, move, and has power with it. The Bible says to "*watch as well as pray*".

Exodus 29:7

"Then shalt thou take the anointing oil, and pour it upon his head, and anoint him".

83

Rochet

Rochet means the head, the top, the upper part, the chief, the total, the sum, the height, the front, the beginning. It starts with the leadership first; don't tell me that you are so highly anointed that you are more anointed than your pastor. I have an entire team called the prophetic cabinet who I have trained to prophesy and speak the word of the Lord; but none of them are more anointed than me. Now, I may have some that could do what I do, but when they are in my house, they must submit their gifts. When you go outside my house, you are free to do your thing. My wife and I had to go through some things in our marriage in order to help other people. So, when you do go through, I understand your pain; because we don't always need to be preached to, sometimes we just need someone to throw their arms around us and tell us it will be alright! The anointed servant has to be in position to receive, because the oil flows from the head. If you are a yielded vessel, the more you yield, the more you can receive. The anointed servant has to be able to see what it is that the leader is preparing to do.

Just because you are close to your leader does not mean you can tell everyone else what to do. You have to know who to tell in order to be effective. This person will usually be the one with the biggest mouth, or the one with the most influence. They may not hold any position in the church, but they hold clout in the eyes of the other parishioners. You can use them, but the leader has to identify when it's expedient to do so, because often the lifestyle of that particular individual may not be a Godly one. I tell my people all the time, just because I don't say anything, does not mean that I don't know. I keep my enemies close so I can see what they are doing. The Bible says "*out of the mouth the heart speaks*" so if I allow you to talk to me long enough, the truth will come out.

The church was not designed to be a democracy, where we vote on the leader, or vote on what happens in the church. When God downloads to me, I feed my sheep. If they are not happy with the meal, there are plenty of other churches to attend. God sends me people who have been designed to be with me, I didn't have to go out soliciting members. The person that did not have a choice in joining is my wife. I'm more concerned about the quality of my ministry, than the quantity of my members. It makes my heart glad when I visit another ministry and they ask one of my leaders to pray or read the scripture. Obedience must also come with leadership, so you cannot do everything that is asked of you, except tithe. You can't say, *I love the preacher, but I just cannot pay my tithes because I am on a fixed income.* For the Bible clearly says, "*Where your treasure is, there is your heart*". So, when I check the records and see that you have not paid your tithes, I'll know that there is a thief in my midst. You may be as sweet as sugar, but I must sit you down because I cannot afford an Achin in the camp. I cannot have you stealing from God talking about you are connected to me; your anointing is starting to disappear because you are not slippery anymore. Your oil has turned into slime.

Are you prepared for the call of purpose that is in your life? When you celebrate God and become yielded vessels, you will begin to dream, see visions, and feel heavy in the middle of the day. It is time for us to stop playing church and become the church; because we have been dealing with the spirit of familiarity. I have some brothers who come to me for prayer; I in turn will ask what he needs prayer for. He might tell me that one of the Sisters is working his nerves. This tells me that I cannot have them working together on an assignment. I am just glad that they can come to me with a situation such as this. Imagine what could happen if I didn't know this, and put the two of them on an assignment together; it's highly possible that they would connect, as spirits do connect. If he is dealing with a lust spirit, and she has one as well, we are going to have a problem.

You may know someone's temperament outside of the house, and have to share it with your leader. *Well Bishop, the brother is alright here, but when he is on the block he drinks alcohol.* I once had a crew in my church that told some new Saints, that I said it was okay to drink alcohol as long as you do not get drunk. They had taken what I said totally out of context, and I became very angry because they uncovered and exposed me to something that I was not a part of. If my wife and I decide to go out and have a glass of wine, that is our business and before the Lord. We may be able to handle it, whereas another person who has had a prior drinking problem cannot; so my wife and I are not going to drink in that individual's presence.

The scripture does talk about wine for the stomachs sake, and yes, Jesus drank wine which was not the grape juice served in church. But, by saying that I said its okay to drink, my people twisted it; because I did not say a thing about Hennessy! I had to come in and teach that holiness is the right way.

Anoint

Mashach (maw-shakh'); to smear, anoint, spread a liquid, to consecrate. When we read in the scripture about the lion, we think of the lion of the tribe of Judah. In the movie, *The Lion King,* the monkey came up when it was time for Simba to be anointed as the new chief, and took liquid from the coconut and smeared it, and anointed him as king. When he got to the top of the rock, the entire kingdom began to bow before the lion (of the tribe of Judah). I got happy in the movie theater because it reminded me of the scripture, *"Every knee shall bow".* There is another cartoon called. *He Man;* when he was normal, he was a prince and his name was Adam, but when he needed to activate his anointing or be strong, he drew his sword and said *"by the powers of gray skull, I have the powers".* Calvary was on Golgotha, the mount of skulls.

Most of us understand that because we enter into the episcopacy we wear garments. The scripture is: Exodus 29:29 *"And the holy garments of Aaron shall be his sons' after him, to be anointed therein, and to be consecrated in them."* We have Bishop consecrations to set them apart for God's use. We lay them prostrate and the men and women of God impart to them. We lay hands on them and touch every part, except the head, which is reserved for the chief celebrant, who is signing off on them stating that the person being consecrated is the one for the job. I am telling you that everyone does not need to lay hands on you, especially when the Bible says *"Lay hands suddenly on no man."* There must be a time when the Bishop comes before his or her peers and speak into their lives and consecrate them. Now that is the legitimacy of the episcopacy. *What about some of the other reformations that do not do consecrations but get voted in?* That is the order of that reformation. Some of the Bishops there will begin to understand the truth, but because of where they are, they go with the flow until the time when they can be in a position to make a change. *Does that make them real Bishops?* Absolutely, because God's hand is on them. Unfortunately, everyone who wears the garments are not exactly who they are supposed to be, you can find no shortage of these people in the news media and by listening to the congregations. The Bible says, "*Be ye transformed by the renewing of your mind*". If we were renewed, we act differently from our former state, and we should be bearing fruit as evidence of that renewal.

Understanding the anointed leader/servant

Usually the servant will ultimately become your leader, and as a servant, God prepares you in boot camp. If I spend enough time with my leader, their traits and habits are going to rub off on me in preparation of my leading someone, somewhere. If you want to know whether you are a leader or not, just turn around and see who is following you. I have a Sister in my church who smokes cigarettes, and if you push the right button, she might even curse you out! But, I notice that she is very funny, and people gravitate to her, so I have not thrown her away for I know what is in her. I've often watched those in my congregation who hang around her start to mimic what she does. Now, if she has this much influence, *why shouldn't I take time out to minister to her and get that junk off so the Lord can use her*? If I were to give her an assignment right now, it would be done in an hour, while the rest of those rabbits will give me excuses. I remember the scripture states that "*The wealth of the wicked is laid up for the just.*" I am not going to put her up to preach, but she is useful in other areas. *Her issue can be seen, but what about your secret, hidden issues*? You don't like your mother and you hate your father; or you steal, you non-tither you! Don't act like you've got it all together, when you are bringing extra pens home from work that you did not buy. "*Thou shalt not steal*".

Brother, when I see you, there's always another new suit you're wearing, but your wife looks shabby. *Doesn't the scripture say that she is your ministry, and that her body is no longer hers and that your body is no longer yours, that you are her provider and protector?* If a man in my church comes in looking sharp and his wife is wearing the same outfit time after time; he is getting called into my office because he is out of order! Either he is going to go out and buy her some new clothes, or I will take her shopping with my wife, because they are representing order. *God takes care of His bride, so why don't you take care of yours?*

I take some of my close leaders to various restaurants because they have to learn to eat foods from other ethnic cultures, so when I go into the fields and take them with me, they won't offend the people we're visiting by refusing to eat their food. If all you know is pulled pork, Bar-B-Q, and fried chicken; you cannot travel with me because my ministry is greater than the South. There are people overseas that need to hear the Word from my mouth, so I must prepare my palate to be accepted in their churches and homes.

Seasons of life in ministry

What season am I in? One of the things that you will suffer is affliction; there will be some sufferings. You will have to die to your own opinion; you may think you know how to do it better, but your leader can see further than you, so you must learn to trust their decisions.

I once had a preacher come to me with a dilemma; he told me that one of his members came to him because someone had given them a winning lottery ticket. I asked him if he wanted me to go to the bank and dance with him! I saw no dilemma there, and I told him that I would put it in the offering and dance and do what God has called me to do. Some may say, that's sinful money, but money does not have a soul, it is a tool! Money will take on the personality of the one who has it. If you are a drunk, you will be in the liquor house with it. But, if you are a child of the King, you will find that money flowing into the church to fulfill the work of the Kingdom. The same dollar that was once in the hand of a drug dealer or a sinner, will eventually wind up in the hand of the mother of the church.

Closing Reflections

I love teaching and traveling the world doing what I do. What is happening is that I am watching servants such as armor bearers, adjutants, and deacons transform. Always inform your Bishop of what you are doing and where you are going. It is not that you are asking permission, but it is always good for your leader to know where you are. For instance, you want to go and visit another ministry to hear another pastor preach. There are some people that your leader would prefer that you not hear, so you are not prone to believe everything that is preached to you. You never know what you can pick up and bring back home.

Bibliography

Spiritual Protocol by Bishop E. Bernard Jordan

Mentoring by Bishop E. Bernard Jordan

The Assignment by Mike Murdock

God's Amourbearers by Terry Nance

Vocati Ad Ministrandum by Bishop J. Delano Ellis

Strong's Concordance

King James Version Bible

Message Version Bible

Developing the Leader With in You by John Maxwell

Servanthood by Bishop E. Bernard Jordan

www.ingramcontent.com/pod-product-compliance
Lightning Source LLC
Chambersburg PA
CBHW051234090426
42740CB00001B/14